Aᴍᴇʀɪᴄᴀ ɪs sᴜFFᴇʀɪɴɢ through two public health crises, one caused by a viral pandemic from halfway around the globe, and the other we've brutally slammed on ourselves.

"Suffering" understates each of these crises. Coronavirus is a vicious disease. Most of us have never before witnessed scenes like the corpses piled up behind hospitals in New York City, the epicenter of the pandemic. The virus's victims, mostly elderly, drown when their lungs fill up with fluid. They die alone, because even their families are barred from visiting their bedside. Their bodies are deposited in bags and forklifted into refrigerator trucks.

Each death is a tragedy, and tens of thousands have already died that way, with more to come.

But the second public health crisis – the shutdown – is almost certain to kill even more Americans. And their deaths will be gruesome, too. Deaths of despair. Leaving behind families who are emotionally broken and destitute.

D0168778

*The shutdown is almost certain
to kill even more Americans
than coronavirus. And they
will be gruesome deaths, too.
Deaths of despair.*

Tens of millions of workers have been laid off because of the government-imposed shutdown. Before the virus hit, America's unemployment rate was 3.5 percent, the lowest in fifty years. Now Goldman Sachs predicts unemployment will be at 15 percent by mid-year. A St. Louis Federal Reserve economist grimly predicts 32 percent unemployment – which is worse than during the Great Depression.

No model or guesswork is required to foresee the deadly impact. Job losses cause extreme suffering. Every 1 percent hike in the unemployment rate will likely produce a 3.3

percent increase in drug overdose deaths and a 0.99 percent increase in suicides, according to data provided by the National Bureau of Economic Research and the medical journal *Lancet*. These are facts based on past experience, not models. If unemployment hits 32 percent, some 77,000 Americans are likely to die from suicide and drug overdoses as a result of layoffs.

Then add the predictable deaths from alcohol abuse caused by unemployment. Ioana Popovici of Nova Southeastern University and Michael French of the University of Miami found a "significant association between job loss ... and binge drinking ... and alcohol abuse."

The impact of layoffs goes beyond suicide, drug overdosing, and drinking. Overall, the death rate for an unemployed person is 63 percent higher than for someone with a job, according to findings in *Social Science & Medicine*.

Not to mention the tragedies of people who spent decades building a small business, only to see it destroyed in weeks because of the shutdown.

Shutdown-related deaths are likely to far outnumber deaths due to coronavirus.

This comparison is not meant to understate the horror of the coronavirus for those who get it and their families. Or to second-guess public officials, who have acted with the best of intentions.

But America should never have to endure another shutdown. The shutdown wasn't caused by the virus. It was a frantic response to America's unpreparedness. The nation's Strategic National Stockpile of medical equipment was nearly empty. Our medical supply chain put us at the mercy of China for masks, antibiotics, and medical supplies. Hospitals were unprepared to stop the spread of infectious diseases. Nursing homes with minimal infection control were destined to become death pits once the virus hit.

The shutdown was originally justified as a way to "flatten the curve," allowing time to expand our health care capacity, so that lives would not be needlessly lost in an overwhelmed, undersupplied system.

The time was well used. Through herculean efforts by governors, the White House, the Federal Emergency Management Agency (FEMA), the US Army Corps of Engineers, the Defense Department, and private-sector companies all across the United States, hospitals in hot zones like New York City got the ventilators they needed and field hospitals took in the patient overflow.

But that begs the question, why was America so unprepared?

Washington politicians can hardly wait to appoint a commission, launch hearings – preferably televised, of course – and piously demand answers to that question. House Intelligence Chairman Adam Schiff and senators Dianne Feinstein and Kamala Harris already have introduced a bill to set up the investigation, claiming the "federal government was unprepared."

They'd like to pin the blame on Donald Trump, but these politicians need to look in the mirror. Nearly every single year for the last two decades, commissions and committees have warned Congress that the medical stockpile was inadequate, our dependence on China was fraught with danger, and our health departments were unready for a pandemic. The Congressional Research Service, the US Government Accountability Office, the Congressional Budget Office, and many others sounded the alarm again and again.

Their findings were ignored, their reports gathered dust, and the very members of Congress who are so outraged now did nothing.

Meanwhile, regardless of who was president, whether a Democrat or a Republican, career federal health bureaucrats ignored America's unpreparedness, while pouring resources into their favorite global projects. They committed billions to fighting Ebola, building health labs and medical training systems on other continents, and conducting disease-fighting programs in forty-nine countries.

In 2015, the Obama administration even

sent $3.7 million of taxpayer money to fund the Wuhan Virology Institute.

While globalism prevailed, preparedness at home faltered.

So here's the message to Washington, DC: No more commissions and televised hearings are needed. It's time to act. This Broadside is a road map for how to battle the next pandemic without a shutdown. It's based on real-time facts on the ground, as the battle against the virus continues.

Many of the steps toward national preparedness listed here are already being taken. The rest are within reach, thanks to the burst of scientific innovation the crisis has inspired.

➤ Stock the US Strategic Stockpile to the brim.

➤ Build a "made-in-America" supply chain for medical supplies.

➤ Level with the public about precautions such as masks.

➤ Improve hospital infection control.

> Don't allow nursing homes to become death pits.

> Get regulators out of the way, so patients have access to treatments.

> Use technology to make workplaces safe from viruses and bacteria.

America ignored the warnings from SARS (severe acute respiratory syndrome), MERS (Middle East respiratory syndrome), the avian flu, and the swine flu. But for the next pandemic, we can be prepared.

Stock the Stockpiles, Retire the Rationers

During the pandemic, working-age people have been worried about missing paychecks, caring for kids home from school, paying for groceries, and cancelling plans. But people in their fifties, sixties, and older have had bigger worries. Many have been lying awake wondering if this is how they're going to die.

At its most severe, coronavirus attacks the lungs, making it impossible to breathe without a ventilator. Landing in the hospital on a ventilator is bad. But worse is being told you can't have one.

When it looked like hospitals in New York were going to run short, Governor Andrew Cuomo complained, "You can't find available ventilators no matter how much you're willing to pay right now because there is literally a global run on ventilators."

It's a little late. Several years ago, after learning that the state's stockpile of medical equipment had 16,000 fewer ventilators than

Regardless of whether we had a Democrat or a Republican president, career federal health bureaucrats ignored America's unpreparedness.

the 18,000 that people living in New York would need in a severe pandemic, Cuomo and state health leaders came to a fork in the road. They could have chosen to buy more ventilators to back up the supplies hospitals maintain. Instead, Cuomo's health commissioner, Howard Zucker, assembled a task force for rationing the ventilators they already had.

In 2015, that task force came up with rules that would be imposed when ventilators ran short. Patients assigned a red code would have highest access, and other patients would be assigned a green, yellow, or blue (the worst) code depending on the decision of a "triage officer." In truth, a death officer. Let's not sugarcoat it. The decision isn't up to your own doctor.

In 2015, Cuomo could have purchased the additional 16,000 ventilators needed for $36,000 apiece, or a total of $576 million. That's a lot of money, but in hindsight, spending one-half of 1 percent of the budget to prepare for a pandemic would have been the right thing to do.

To be fair, many state governments made the same mistake, and stockpiled few or no ventilators. And yes, they also wrote ghoulish plans for who would get one, either then or when the pandemic arrived.

The federal Strategic National Stockpile was also undersupplied with ventilators to meet the coronavirus emergency.

Then the pandemic arrived. Noted rationer Dr. Ezekiel Emanuel, once an advisor to President Obama, cowrote an article in the *New England Journal of Medicine* putting forward his concept of fairness.

New York City's deputy commissioner for disease control, Demetre Daskalakis, said he anticipated "some very serious difficult decisions."

Arthur Caplan, a bioethicist at NYU Langone Medical Center, said there is no single "right" answer about who gets a ventilator. With all due respect, there is a right answer: Everyone who needs one.

In Wuhan, China, doctors recently faced the grim arithmetic of 1,000 patients needing ventilators and only 600 ventilators being available. Italy is rationing ventilators, too.

But in the United States of America, rationing ventilators should be unnecessary. State and local hospitals knew of the shortage, had the money, and should have bought the lifesaving equipment, instead of making a plan on who would live and die.

Lesson to the bioethicists in universities across this country who like to write rationing rules: Americans don't want their government holding back on the things they need to stay alive.

That's a lesson everyone – except the bioethicists – agreed on when the pandemic arrived. Even Cuomo said he found it abhorrent to deny any single person a ventilator.

Fortunately, the Trump administration did something about it, swinging into action to marshal the private sector to ramp up ventilator production. "There's been no American that has needed a ventilator that has not received one," announced Adam Boehler,

CEO of the US International Development Finance Corporation, in mid-April.

In the year prior to the pandemic, according to administration figures, the United States produced 30,000 ventilators. In 2020, it's going to produce 200,000.

Better yet, the Trump administration has worked with the American Hospital Association and the Federation of American Hospitals to design a system where in any future pandemic or health crisis, hospitals can borrow and lend ventilators. It's called the Dynamic Ventilator Reserve. All over the nation, top hospital centers are joining the system, including the Mayo Clinic and the Cleveland Clinic. A digital clearinghouse will track where the needs and surpluses are.

Under the terms of the plan, if a hospital lends out ventilators and then is hit with an emergency need, its ventilators will be replaced within hours. America will be ready with ventilators for the next respiratory pandemic.

In 2015, Cuomo could have purchased the additional 16,000 ventilators needed for $576 million. Spending 0.5 percent of the budget to prepare for the pandemic would have been the right thing to do.

The ventilator shortage exposed a bigger problem: For two decades, Congress and the federal health bureaucracy were warned again and again that not enough medical supplies were on hand in the event of a pandemic. They were told during three successive presidencies, when both Democrats and Republicans were in office.

In 2003, after the SARS outbreak, the US Government Accountability Office cautioned that hospitals lacked the capacity and equipment, including ventilators, to handle a major respiratory outbreak.

The Congressional Research Service issued a report warning of unpreparedness in 2005. The Congressional Budget Office followed with another report in 2006. The Department of the Interior sounded the alarm in 2007. And on and on.

The last thing needed now is another commission, congressional hearing, or report. The CDC, which was in charge of the National Strategic Stockpile until two years ago, failed to ask for sufficient funding for it.

The agency wasn't shy about requesting and getting over $4 billion to fund health care infrastructure and training sent overseas during and after the Ebola crisis, or another half a billion for health programs in forty-nine countries. The CDC ought to be called the "Centers for Disbursement of Cash to Foreign Countries."

At the same time it was spending money overseas, the federal government was steadily reducing funding for state and local health departments in the United States. That left these departments totally unprepared to handle the Zika virus challenge in 2016, and without the lab capacity or staffing to respond to the coronavirus pandemic.

Blame the federal bureaucracy's inveterate globalism. The lesson is fund public health and lab capacity in our own country first.

Even now, as Americans strain to come up with enough resources to fight coronavirus and survive an economic shutdown, the former CDC director under the Obama administration, Tom Frieden, is urging us to spend more in other countries. He wants American taxpayers to "fill thousands of life-threatening gaps in disease preparedness worldwide" and "commit to global solidarity."

That's precisely the viewpoint that left American public health systems unprepared and underfunded for this pandemic.

Level with the Public about Masks

New York, New Jersey, Maryland, and other states are requiring everyone to wear a mask or a substitute face covering when leaving their home. The federal Centers for Disease Control and Prevention has suddenly flipped from urging the public not to wear masks to recommending that everyone wear a face cloth covering in public.

The new signature look of New York's mayor, Bill de Blasio, is a Western-style bandanna pulled up over his mouth and nose. No doubt he's well intentioned. But that kind of face covering is only a hair better than no covering at all. Science shows it's a mere 2–3 percent effective. It's misleading.

From day one of the coronavirus outbreak, the public has gotten the runaround about masks. Government officials need to be honest about what works and what doesn't. Here's the scientific evidence:

> **N95 masks:** These are molded to the face and fit tight, filtering out 95 percent of viral particles, even the smallest ones. These masks offer the best protection, but they are in short supply, and public

officials want them reserved for health care workers on the front lines.

> **Surgical masks:** Commonly worn in hospitals and dentists' offices, these masks are flat and held to the face with elastic. They're made from a nonwoven material, polypropylene, and act as a somewhat effective filter. They protect the wearer from about 56 percent of viral droplets emitted by an infected person nearby, according to research in the *British Medical Journal.*

> **Not-so-woven cloth masks:** These masks allow in 97 percent of viral particles. That means almost no protection for the wearer at all.

> **Homemade cotton masks:** Wearing these masks is a false assurance, explains epidemiologist May Chu. She says they block only about 2 percent of airflow. Similarly, a study in *Disaster Medicine and Public Health Preparedness* concludes that a

homemade mask should "only be considered as a last resort" – better than no protection at all, but not a lot better.

Surgical masks are available in stores now, and if you can buy a supply, using them is far preferable to making your own. Just be sure not to reuse the mask and avoid touching the outside of the mask, because it's likely to be contaminated after use.

If you have to resort to homemade barriers, keep in mind that the more layers of cloth, the better the protection. Four layers likely block out 13 percent of viral droplets, compared with the 2 percent blocked with a single layer, according to a study in *Aerosol and Air Quality Research.*

Why are public officials suddenly urging mask use, so many weeks after the coronavirus struck? Because of mounting research pointing to the huge role of asymptomatic people spreading the disease before they feel ill. Whenever these asymptomatic carriers talk or simply exhale, they spread very small droplets of virus-laden saliva and respiratory mucous in the air. Scientists call these bioaerosols.

Getting everyone to mask up does a double duty: It helps to protect the uninfected and it keeps the unknowingly infected from spreading the virus. As Governor Cuomo said, announcing the mask mandate: "You don't have a right to infect me."

Makes sense, but Americans have had to put up with a lot of message confusion from the outset, and now they're getting misleading advice about homemade masks.

What's the root problem? Year after year after year, through three presidencies, federal health bureaucrats ignored warnings about inadequate supplies of masks and other equipment in the event of a pandemic. Ten federal reports sounded the alarm, as the nation witnessed SARS, MERS, the avian flu, and the swine flu circle the globe. In 2009, during the swine flu outbreak, the federal Strategic National Stockpile dispersed

> *Nurses and first responders in the United States are begging for PPE, and China's watching at a distance, no doubt enjoying the spectacle.*

eighty-five million N95 masks, as well as other protective masks. The masks were never replaced afterward.

Don't blame any president, Democratic or Republican, for this oversight. The career officials at the Department of Health & Human Services knowingly allowed the nation to be undersupplied. They never requested enough money to adequately stock the Strategic National Stockpile, according to the stockpile's former director, Greg Burel, who retired in January.

HHS requested a mere $595–$705 million

a year, with the highest request coming during Trump's tenure.

Their agenda was global. But no masks for Americans.

When the coronavirus struck here, the CDC offered only mask double-talk. The agency said on the one hand masks are vital to protect health care workers, and on the other hand masks won't make the public safer. It defies common sense. The agency should have leveled with people, admitting that the supplies had to be saved for front-line caregivers.

The coronavirus could return next winter. Or another viral pandemic could strike from any part of the globe. The bill Congress enacted in late March allocates $16 billion to the Strategic National Stockpile, nearly thirty times its previous annual budgets. Next time, the United States will have enough masks.

A Made-in-America
Medical Supply Chain

America needs a reliable medical supply chain to be prepared for a pandemic.

Federal health bureaucrats deserve an *F* grade for ignoring this. Despite years of warnings about America's overdependence on China for medicines, masks, and medical equipment, these officials failed to remedy the situation. They dithered through several presidencies, Democratic and Republican alike.

Now these officials are telling us we are in a public health crisis from coronavirus. Bad enough if we had the weapons to fight it, but this virus caught us with our proverbial pants down. Senator Ron Johnson of Wisconsin told the Senate Homeland Security and Governmental Affairs Committee: "It's quite shocking to me that we have allowed this to happen." Shocking? It's government as usual.

During the past decade, congressional hearings, special commissions, and thousands of pages of reports have documented the danger of relying on China for life-and-death medical supplies. It's been all talk, and almost no action.

China is the number-one supplier of surgical masks, protective goggles, plastic gloves, and generic antibiotics like tetracycline, and the number-two source of mechanical ventilators, hand sanitizer, alcohol solution, and other essential supplies.

Experts warned that if China-US relations soured, China could cut off antibiotic exports and other medical supplies, throwing our hospitals into turmoil.

That's exactly what's happened. In early February 2020, the Chinese nationalized production and dissemination of medical supplies, including seizing control of what US companies produce there and diverting it for domestic use only. Firms like 3M, Foxconn, and General Motors were ordered to produce significant amounts of personal protective equipment (PPE), including face masks, all for Chinese consumption.

China's actions worsened shortages in the United States.

Then the political games began. In April, China imposed new restrictions on exports of medical goods, insisting it was for quality control purposes. Companies ready to export face masks, ventilators, and other equipment, like PerkinElmer, had their products held up in warehouses waiting for newly required Chinese go-aheads, according to the Congressional Research Service.

Nurses and first responders in the United States are begging for PPE, and China's watching at a distance, no doubt enjoying the spectacle.

Just to show how out to lunch the federal bureaucracy is about putting globalism ahead of American safety, the State Department issued a press release on February 7 proudly announcing that it was facilitating an airlift to China of $18 million worth of PPE donated by the private sector to alleviate the crisis there. As the Congressional Research Service notes, that "further deplet[ed] U.S. supplies."

It's hard to overstate the suffering and lives put at risk by the shortage of this equipment.

But the lesson is that the United States must correct its dependence on China for the medicines and medical supplies we need to stay alive.

Even without the coronavirus pandemic, this should have been done years ago.

Our dependence is a national security risk. We wouldn't depend on China for fighter planes or aircraft carriers. The federal US-China Economic and Security Review Commission warned about the dangers of American reliance on China for life-saving drugs. If the United States were attacked with anthrax, China would be a major source of ciprofloxacin, an antibiotic needed to treat victims. But what if China were the attacker, one expert warned?

The commission also warned about the "serious deficiencies in health and safety standards" in Chinese drug factories. In short, the squalid conditions.

The FDA has a long history of failing to oversee foreign drug sources, according to scathing reports from the Government Accountability Office. In the United States, pharmaceutical plants are inspected every two years. In China, some never get inspected.

In 2008, a contaminated blood thinner from China, heparin, killed eighty-one American patients. Heparin is made from the mucous membranes of pig intestines. In China, slaughtered pigs are often cooked in unregulated family work spaces as a first step in the drug-manufacturing process. It's a cottage industry.

The FDA initially concluded that the contaminated heparin came from a Chinese factory using unclean storage tanks. But later the agency changed its view, and suspected intentional contamination.

Chinese authorities, meanwhile, responded only with denials and more denials. The reason the FDA had little chance to uncover the contamination before Americans started dying: It had not inspected the plant. Even now, it has only thirty-nine staff members dedicated to inspecting more than 3,000 foreign manufacturing facilities.

Heparin is just one example of what can go wrong. A more recent example is blood pressure medications with the active ingredient valsartan. The FDA has had to announce over

---

If there's a silver lining, it's the pressure to end our dependence on China and build a made-in-America medical and pharmaceutical supply chain.

---

fifty recalls of blood pressure medications because the valsartan in them contained jet fuel contaminants estimated to cause cancer in one out of every 8,000 pill takers. Who supplies these medications? China.

The FDA advised that it's less risky for a

person to take the contaminated pill than to skip taking blood pressure medications. Yikes. Patients shouldn't have to face that choice.

If there's a silver lining in the coronavirus pandemic, it's the pressure to end our dependence on China and build a made-in-America medical and pharmaceutical supply chain.

Motivated to help America in this time of crisis, businesses large and small innovated, converting their manufacturing operations to meet medical needs. As the *Wall Street Journal* reported, True Value converted part of its paint factory into a facility to make hand sanitizer. General Motors teamed up with Ventec Life Systems to make ventilators. Just proof that there are plenty of manufacturers in the United States that could add medical supplies to their product lineup.

Message to Governor Andrew Cuomo in New York: Here's a way to revitalize the stagnant upstate economy and meet a real need, instead of pouring money into boondoggle "job-creation" projects like the Buffalo Bill solar panels funded by state taxpayers.

Congress is already looking at ways to remedy the reliance on foreign suppliers after the pandemic. But lawmakers have to think bigger. So far, the bills would add layers of paperwork requirements for pharma and medical supply manufacturers to report foreign supply chain vulnerabilities. A typical Washington, DC, approach. Instead, Congress needs to create tax incentives to bring manufacturing home.

The Trump administration is making building an American supply chain a top priority. It is pledging $421 million toward Johnson & Johnson's $1 billion project to manufacture a coronavirus vaccine here in the United States.

No matter where a viral pandemic originates, the tools to fight it need to be made in America.

Improving Hospital Infection Control

Johns Hopkins doctors are cautioning that the hospital could become a "disease amplifier," spreading the coronavirus to health care workers, visitors, and patients who didn't come in with it. Truth is, that's already happening.

The key to preparing for the next pandemic, or a return of the coronavirus, is to improve infection control in hospitals.

Health care workers — the heroes in the coronavirus pandemic — are bearing the brunt. Nearly one out of every five infected Americans is a health care worker, according to a CDC report. The root causes are lax infection control standards, equipment shortages, and inadequate training.

Typical is what happened on February 15, when someone unknowingly infected with the virus went to a hospital in Solano County, California, for help. For four days, doctors and nurses and other hospital workers interacted with patient zero, performing exams and inserting breathing devices without wearing any PPE-like face masks, gowns, or masks. No surprise that three of these medical personnel became infected.

That same scenario is being repeated all across the United States. On March 3, an Uber driver walked into the St. John's Episcopal Hospital emergency room in Queens, New York. He complained of flu-like symptoms, but the staff sent him home. He returned sicker a few hours later. By the time he was put in isolation, up to forty doctors, nurses, and other hospital staff had had contact with him and were forced to go into isolation. Worse, the incident also exposed numerous hospital visitors and other patients to danger.

Fortunately, in regions being pummeled by the coronavirus, hospitals are on alert, and have set up separate emergency areas for suspected cases. But that precaution will be short-lived. To prepare for the next pandemic, or a return of the coronavirus at a later date, health care professionals need rigorous training in how to identify a possibly infectious patient, when and how to don protective gear, and how to avoid self-contamination. In the aftermath of the current pandemic, hospitals should be conducting boot camp drills.

Hospitals had years of warning that their staffs were not ready for a pandemic, and that unpreparedness could cost many lives.

In 2003, when SARS, also a coronavirus, struck Ontario, Canada, 77 percent of the people infected with the virus contracted it in the hospital. They were patients, visitors, and health care workers. It started as an infection brought from Asia by a traveler, but rapidly became a hospital infection.

A Toronto man whose mother had just returned from Hong Kong was feeling ill and went to the hospital with feverish symptoms. For sixteen hours, he was kept in a packed

If hospitals can't control the spread of these bacteria, how will they contain a viral infection that spreads not only on surfaces but also in particles in the air?

emergency room. His virus infected the man in the adjacent bed, who had come to the ER with heart problems, and another man three beds away with shortness of breath. Staff failed to wear masks and disposable gowns, and didn't wear face shields while inserting a breathing tube down the patient's throat. A report by the Government of Ontario later concluded that the disease spread fast through the hospital because "infection control was not a priority."

In any future pandemic, the public's safety and the well-being of health care workers will depend on what happens when a patient who is unknowingly carrying a contagion walks into an emergency room for help. That will be patient zero.

Hospitals here in the United States were alerted again and again that they were not ready before the pandemic struck. The Centers for Disease Control and Prevention conducted "mystery patient" drills at ERs in forty-nine New York City area hospitals, sending in patients pretending to have measles or MERS. In 22 percent of cases, the ER staff failed to isolate these patients and give them masks to wear. Only 36 percent of health care staff washed their hands. The CDC found "suboptimal adherence to key infection control practices."

We owe health care workers more rigorous training than that.

The high rate of coronavirus infections among health care workers and the dangers posed to their families are producing heightened awareness that things have to change.

Health care workers who used to wear their scrubs and hospital footwear out onto the street, into restaurants, and even home to their children are taking new precautions. In New York City, hundreds of health care workers are using donated hotel rooms or sleeping in their cars to avoid spreading the virus to their families.

This is an important lesson for the future. Hospitals used to provide laundered scrubs for their personnel and locker rooms for changing. That should be done again. Research in

Emerging Infectious Diseases shows that, half the time, the soles of shoes worn by personnel in ICUs that treat coronavirus patients are contaminated with the virus.

Hospitals also need to consider installing lids on toilets. One of the highest concentrations of coronavirus traces was found in public restrooms. The virus is carried in fecal matter, and when toilets are flushed it can become aerosolized, just like the common bacterial infection *Clostridium difficile.* To protect patients and caregivers alike, toilets need lids that can be closed before flushing.

The extensive research on how long the coronavirus survives on surfaces is directing new, urgently needed attention to the ways infections race through hospitals on inadequately cleaned wheelchairs, blood pressure cuffs, bed rails, computer keyboards, and other items.

The truth is that at least 72,000 hospital patients die each year from bacterial infections, usually caused by unclean hands, inadequately cleaned equipment, and lax procedures. If hospitals can't control the spread of these bacteria – and death statistics prove they can't – how will they manage to contain a viral infection that spreads not only on surfaces but also in droplets and aerosolized particles in the air?

Now is the time for a nationwide campaign to improve infection control in hospitals. If we are spared a return of the coronavirus or another pandemic, better infection control will save tens of thousands of lives a year. It's a no-brainer.

The Most Dangerous Place to Be Is in a Nursing Home

The most dangerous place to be during the coronavirus pandemic isn't a cruise ship, the subway, or even a crowded theater. The riskiest place to be is in a nursing home or rehab center. They're ground zero for the coronavirus.

As of mid-April, 58 percent of Delaware's coronavirus deaths were of nursing home residents; in Massachusetts, they made up 55 percent of the coronavirus deaths; in Pennsylvania, it was 51 percent; and in New Jersey, 40 percent.

When the coronavirus first struck, officials turned a blind eye to nursing homes, or worse, tried to keep the soaring deaths happening in them secret.

Correcting the deplorable lack of infection control in nursing homes and supplying needed masks, gowns, and other PPE to these facilities could cut this nation's overall coronavirus death rate by double digits. Not by half, of course, because the elderly are vulnerable to this respiratory disease, and some will die from it, no matter how expert and timely the care.

When another respiratory pandemic that affects the elderly reaches the United States, or the coronavirus returns, the nation should be ready to rush equipment and added staff to nursing homes. Go where the risk of fatalities is greatest.

The carnage at Life Care Center nursing

home in Kirkland, Washington, should have been a warning. Since the first Life Care patient tested positive on February 28, 167 people there have contracted the virus, including 101 residents, fifty staff members, and sixteen visitors, forty-three of whom have died.

Some of the caregivers at Life Care worked at other nursing homes, too, and brought the disease to the other locations. At the outset, infected patients weren't given masks to wear, even when they were being transported to a nearby hospital. As staff fell ill, nursing care was stretched thinner. Kirkland turned out to be a preview of what would happen across the nation.

Coronavirus races through nursing homes, with a mortality rate of nearly 20 percent, reports Dr. Richard Feifer, chief medical officer at Genesis Health Care.

New York State, the epicenter of the coronavirus, accounts for roughly 60 percent of the nation's nursing home deaths, according to *NBC News*.

"Coronavirus in a nursing home can be

like fire through dry grass," explains Governor Cuomo.

At one Brooklyn nursing home, the situation is so dire that deceased residents are left in their beds after death. There's no place else to store the bodies. A nurse there told the *New York Post*, "It's so sad to be taking blood from someone and the person in the next bed – next to them – is dead."

New Jersey has also been hard hit. "When we do the national and New Jersey post mortem [on the epidemic,] long-term-care facilities are going to be at the top of the list," says New Jersey governor Phil Murphy.

There's no need to wait until the pandemic's over. Now's the time to prepare for the next wave of infectious disease.

The Centers for Disease Control and Prevention analyzed what went wrong at Life Care. It determined that the staff were unfamiliar with rigorous infection control, including how to safely put on and remove a mask without infecting themselves and how to recognize when a patient might be infected and require isolation. Infection control tools, like hand sanitizer, gowns, and masks, were in short supply.

No surprises there. Even in good times, when the nation is undergoing a pandemic, nursing homes are cauldrons of infection. It is no exaggeration to say most facilities ignore precautions like keeping infected residents apart from others, and disinfecting rooms and medical equipment.

A staggering 380,000 nursing home residents a year die from infections with names we've all come to dread, like MRSA (methicillin-resistant *Staphylococcus aureus*), VRE (vancomycin-resistant *enterococcus*), and C. diff (*Clostridium difficile*), as well as various pneumonias. Not all are preventable. The low standards of prevention for infection largely accounts for the toll. Residents with staph are rolled into communal dining rooms and seated next to other residents. Super-bugs contaminate bed rails, curtains, and rehab equipment. Caregivers tasked with bathing and grooming residents go from one bed to the next without donning disposable gowns and gloves, spreading bacteria and viruses as they go.

One-quarter of nursing home residents pick up dangerous, drug-resistant bacteria, according to Columbia University School of Nursing research.

Nursing home residents are sitting ducks for a viral pandemic like the coronavirus.

To make matters worse, in some states officials refused to disclose which nursing homes are affected.

But the biggest mistake is what New York State did. In March, as hospitals there were inundated with patients and short on bed capacity, the state mandated that any nursing home must accept coronavirus patients being discharged from a hospital and prohibited the nursing facility from asking for a COVID-19 test prior to admission or readmission.

Despite enormous pushback from patient advocates, the state has stuck to its position. It's probably a well-meaning attempt to bar "discrimination" against infected patients. But the number-one rule of infection control is to diagnose and isolate. The New York

Private-sector companies have been pounding on doors for years with lifesaving technologies trying to get the attention of federal bureaucrats, who have ingrained suspicion of the private sector.

mandate does just the opposite: it conceals who has the disease and mandates its spread.

Connecticut and Massachusetts designated certain facilities for coronavirus patients in order to keep other facilities virus-free. When St. Joseph's Senior Home in New Jersey became overwhelmed by an outbreak, Care-One came to the rescue, taking in all the St.

Joseph's patients, dedicating an entire facility to the coronavirus, and transferring virus-free patients to another building. That's the right idea.

Florida's governor, Ron DeSantis, also deserves kudos. Health officials in New York and most states rushed to equip hospitals for the coronavirus but ignored nursing homes. Without help, these facilities became cauldrons of death. But DeSantis hurried medical supplies to nursing homes in his state, deployed the National Guard to test residents, and cut the nursing home death rate to roughly half that of New York.

On April 2, the Centers for Medicare & Medicaid Services (CMS) at long last issued new guidelines targeting the huge number of deaths in nursing homes. CMS is urging state and local officials to prioritize getting PPE and other infection-control supplies to these facilities.

Had European countries followed that strategy, they could have avoided the tragic death tolls they are facing. In Italy, 53 percent of deaths were of nursing home residents, in Spain it was 57 percent, and in Ireland 54 percent.

What's the lesson for the next pandemic or the return of coronavirus later in the year? Improve infection control in nursing homes. The federal government rates nursing homes on a one-to-five-star scale based on periodic inspections, staffing levels, and infection rates. But even nursing homes that get the lowest one-star rating year after year are allowed to stay open. They should be shut down.

And when a contagion threatens, we need to have a plan in place to rush additional resources to nursing homes. They were just an afterthought in this first pandemic. Nursing homes are where the help will be needed and the most lives will be saved.

REASON FOR OPTIMISM

President Trump told the Food and Drug Administration to "slash red tape like nobody's ever done before." That message is getting to every federal regulatory agency, and the result will be a burst of technological improvements in workplace safety, hospital hygiene, and medical cures.

Private-sector companies all across the nation are responding to the pandemic by developing new products and services. Truth is, they've been pounding on doors for years with lifesaving technologies trying to get the attention of federal bureaucrats, who have ingrained suspicion of the private sector.

If you're an academic scientist or work in a government lab, you can talk to federal regulators any day of the week. But if you work for a for-profit company, you can only get an audience of these regulators on "vendor day." As if you're tainted. That's changing, thanks to the pandemic.

Agencies like the FDA and the CDC need to be more flexible, less risk-averse, and more open to innovation when so many lives are at stake. That was the lesson, after the CDC tried to make its own coronavirus test and the FDA dragged its feet on approving tests devised by private and state laboratories.

Rapid Point-of-Care Testing

In the end, private companies like Cepheid and Abbott came through with rapid tests that provide results in a few minutes or a few hours, rather than days. Here's the long-term dividend. After the enthusiasm shown for rapid coronavirus testing, expect hospitals to start using rapid tests for MRSA, strep, the lethal fungal infection *Candida auris*, and other pathogens. Faster answers will save lives and reduce the use of incorrect antibiotics.

The technology has existed for several years to provide testing for many infectious agents at a patient's bedside or in a doctor's office using molecular methods, instead of sending a culture to the lab and waiting days for the results. But hospitals have been painfully slow to adopt it.

If you go to most hospital emergency rooms with an infection, they'll take a culture and tell you you'll get an answer in two to three days. In the meantime, they're flying blind, prescribing an antibiotic without being sure it's the best choice. That's about to change for the better. The coronavirus is pushing hospitals into the twenty-first century.

Better Infection Control in Hospitals

Nowhere is technological innovation more needed than in infection prevention. Dreaded bacterial infections like MRSA and C. diff kill over 70,000 hospital patients a year in the United States. It's amazing but true that one

Patients with cancer, heart disease, and other illnesses cannot access breakthrough treatments if infection makes going into the hospital too risky.

of the largest causes of death in our country is something the hospital gives you.

That's why I founded the Committee to Reduce Infection Deaths. RID educates patients and caregivers on the steps they can take to reduce their risk and brings the latest research to hospital decision makers on what they can do to shield patients from risk.

Patients with cancer, heart disease, and other illnesses cannot access breakthrough treatments if infection makes going into the hospital too risky. All the benefits of medical science – from joint replacement to chemotherapy – depend on being able to prevent the spread of hospital infections.

Lax infection control is taking a terrible toll on health care workers during the pandemic. The CDC advises health care workers to "take care of yourself and follow recommended infection control protocols." Truth is, those protocols are not rigorous enough, even in ordinary times, and hygiene in hospitals is deficient.

Despite following those protocols, doctors

and nurses routinely spread bacterial infections from patient to patient, even at a prestigious hospital like Johns Hopkins.

Hospital cleaning is hit and miss. A study of 1,100 hospital rooms from Washington, DC, to Boston showed that on average, cleaning staff overlooked half the surfaces in these rooms, including the over-the-bed tables and bed rails. If you have to eat your lunch in a hospital room, it's probably safest to put your sandwich on the toilet seat. That always gets cleaned.

Professor William Rutala at the University of North Carolina School of Medicine, an expert on infection prevention, cautions that the manual cleaning of hospital rooms "does not adequately disinfect." Contaminated beds and mattresses, privacy curtains, and medical equipment allow infections to race through hospitals.

To be prepared for the next pandemic, and to improve patient and health care staff safety from day to day, hospitals need to take fuller advantage of new technologies: antimicrobial fabrics; copper and copper-impregnated polymers for bed rails, keyboards, and other medical equipment; and high-tech methods of disinfection, including UV light, hydrogen peroxide misting, and automatic continuous disinfection using dry hydrogen peroxide.

Safer Workplaces

Reopening the economy will hinge on making employees feel safe at work. Many companies are scrambling to hire cleaning crews to scrub desktops, keyboards, doorknobs, and other frequently touched surfaces. But that's somewhat futile, because as soon as someone unknowingly carrying the virus sneezes, or touches a keyboard, the surfaces will be recontaminated.

One answer is continuous, nontoxic automatic disinfection. Technologies to achieve that already exist. For example, an American company in the Kansas City area, Synexis, on whose board I serve, makes a device installed in a building's HVAC system that continuously deactivates viruses in the air and eradicates bacteria, funguses, and mold on surfaces using dry hydrogen peroxide at such diluted levels that it poses no danger to human beings.

It's EPA approved. And it's already widely used in fast food outlets, food storage, and poultry production, where it eliminates the need for antibiotics. Now, with the pandemic, it promises to make workplaces safer, too.

Safer Airports

Pandemics are spread by travelers. MIT researchers found that improving hand hygiene at the world's top ten airports could curb the spread of infectious disease by 37 percent. How to do that? Install hand sanitizer stands next to check-in kiosks, at the end of jetways where passengers can use them as they deplane, and at security checkpoints. Making hand sanitizers routine at all airports would reduce the risk of a pandemic by 70 percent.

Our victory against coronavirus and future viral attacks will depend on new cures. There is a palpable sense of urgency in the pharma and biotech world to discover them. Now it's up to regulators to provide real-time reviews of how well these experimental drugs are working, instead of waiting for trials to conclude. And to grant compassionate use, so that no patients are denied a chance at life.

There is reason for optimism as we battle this pandemic and prepare for future global disease assaults.

The virus struck only months ago, and already we know its genetic features. It took scientists years to get that far with HIV. The pace of scientific progress is breathtaking.

Most important, our nation will be prepared for the next pandemic. No shutdown necessary.

The Committee to Reduce Infection Deaths offers employers, government, and hospital decision-makers information on the best technologies to beat COVID-19 in the workplace, including antimicrobial coatings, keyboards, desktops and furnishings, no-touch doors, copper pushplates and handrails, and continuous disinfection of air and surfaces. Please visit our website at hospitalinfection .org and request our brochure: 8 Steps to Beating COVID in the Workplace.

First American edition published in 2020 by Encounter Books, an activity of Encounter for Culture and Education, Inc., a nonprofit, tax exempt corporation. Encounter Books website address: www.encounterbooks.com

Manufactured in the United States and printed on acid-free paper. The paper used in this publication meets the minimum requirements of ANSI / NISO Z39.48–1992 (R 1997) (*Permanence of Paper*).

FIRST AMERICAN EDITION

LIBRARY OF CONGRESS CATALOGING-IN-PUBLICATION DATA IS AVAILABLE